Haunted.
Evaporations
by Toby Chown

dopLin

First published in February 2018 by Doplin Books, Brighton
Find us on Facebook @doplinbooks

Production Editor: Xanna Eve Chown

Cover design by Tom Kington
Cover photograph by the author

ISBN-13: 978-1546574002

For Rubytulip and Bonnie

Special thanks to Tanya Shadrick, Gemma Kauffman, Steve Thorpe, Xanna Eve Chown, Tom Kington and Kassia Zermon for help kindling and guarding the secret flame, and so keeping the art life alive.

Contents

Preface

Reading these poems brings eternity to the front door, as if it's the most natural and humble guest...

If you, like myself, sometimes wish there was a fast-track to unfolding the great mysteries of life - a button you could press that would explode the depth of existence into something more tangible, maybe something you can wear, try on, take off, try on again, look in the mirror and not feel foolish about wearing clothes that are way too big - then you too, will find gold in these lines.

   Haunted is an offering of many layers, a different gift for each new level of awareness that inevitably expands from one reading to the next. Toby is able to channel a timeless voice that sharpens perception and steers attention, bypassing analysis and entering the body like a fine, weightless mist.

   As these strange times unravel, I've became increasingly grateful to have a window into the poems of *Haunted*, each one an invitation to face yourself through the lens of the ancient, the mythic and the psychic. Yes, the poems are as delicate as a spider's thread, but be prepared to be floored, struck, to feel time stop, to deeply inhale and then exhale as if you have just woken up, and in doing so, be forced to recognise that despite your best efforts to forget, you are indeed, for a moment at least, truly and blissfully alive.

- Gemma Kauffman, Artist, Director of Dream of Life CIC

Hauntings

'Time is nature's way of preventing everything from happening at once.'
- *John Archibald Wheeler*

Being haunted

It is not so much the *reality* of ghosts that matters to me in this book, but the idea of being haunted as a shorthand for the poetics of memories and feelings.

What does it mean to be haunted? We can use the word to describe being haunted by a ghost, as well as by a feeling or memory - as if feelings and memories are ghosts, with a life of their own.

A common explanation for ghosts is that they are the psychic residues of people with feelings so strong that they couldn't help leaving an image of themselves behind after death. But if ghosts are our ancestors, why are we scared of them? They could just as easily means us well. We, too, are ghosts, after all. Our lives have an ephemeral quality and we are often invisible to each other.

The idea that past and future are illusions - and that *now* is the only time there is - has haunted me since I was a child. If *now* is always happening, then perhaps our deaths have in some sense already happened. That moment too, happens *now*. We are bound to become ghosts to our own children and grandchildren, one day. In this case we should know the message we want to pass on.

The return of the ghosts

The psychologist Carl Jung begins his *Seven Sermons to the Dead* like this: 'The dead came back from Jerusalem, where they found not what they sought.'

The sermon deals with something we overlook in our modern lives: The extent to which the world we find ourselves living in is not a reflection of our own desires, but the realisation of the flawed desires of our ancestors.

The dead can find no rest in the holy city, just as Christian theology could no longer comfort Jung.

Today, it can feel like we have little rest either. The binding structures of Christianity theology that Jung sought to revitalise have long given way to a fragmented, jarring world, somehow both neon and grey.

We judder between a blindly reductive, yet dominant materialistic scientism, and a disconnected, yet skillfully subversive postmodern identity. Our science and postmodern ennui leave us lost in self-referential symbolism, mistaking our minds for the real world in more and cleverer ways, haunting the internet for words of comfort or connection.

Mythic patterns in everyday narrative

Yet, life is not simply defined by alienation or fragmentation, and human beings are not only the victims of an uncaring reality. Reality has more to offer than measurement of matter or an endless reflections in digital mirrors.

There is another tradition, hidden below the surface of western thought, of a poetic basis of mind, of the mythic patterns within everyday experiences, of traces of a greater whole. Bearing this in mind, the poems in the first section are not about being haunted by ghosts - but by gods.

Jung wrote that the gods had been banished from reality into our interior life, where we experience them as symptoms, problems, disowned parts of ourselves. The writer, Alan Moore, commented that if the gods exist anywhere, it is in our imagination.

Yet, perhaps now more than ever, we misunderstand the imagination too, seeing it too as something inside us, a form of entertainment and escapism.

How much harder this makes grasping imagination as a way of seeing and understanding our own lives and our own world! Yet how important it seems to grasp this now, split between post-truth politics and industrial economics, our lives reconstituted as 'narratives' - with our selves, rather than gods or ghostly ancestors the authors - medicated against our own moods, trapped in the safe zone of an industrial world that lets us have our stories and make our art so long as these things do not interfere with the real business, of, well, business.

The gods

'The gods have become diseases,' wrote Jung. A darker vision of gods, not as fantasies but as pathologies, as ways of imagining the forces that interfere with our own desires, a name for unacknowledged forces behind our most difficult experiences.

This seems a lot like being haunted, this way of imagining the gods.

They haunt us with those aspects of our lives that we refuse to see. The ivy of Dionysos flourishes in abandoned places, cemeteries and walls. It demonstrates the invisible, relentless vitality of nature, growing in the face of death and technology.

We live in a culture afraid of death, and with no cosmology to make sense of the thresholds of life and death.

A friend once said to me, 'death is a stone.' I think he meant death seemed impersonal, inanimate, unrelatable. Yet, the lyre of Orpheus sings of grief and love as utterly entwined. The trickster Hermes's snake-entwined staff guides the way between worlds, encourages us to accept the paradoxes and contradictions of life.

It may yet turn out that our grief is the best guide we have to how to live in a world laced with inevitable sorrow.

We live in an age of fragmentation, medication, depression and uncertainty. Can we accept that stories might not be pretty projections that flicker on our living-room walls, but pathways forged out of thousands of years of psychological struggle, archetypes for a pathway through?

Perhaps myth is not meant to enchant us, but to wake us up, to remind us of what we have forgotten. Whether the denial is of death, of depression, of ecology, of the feminine, the gods continue to haunt us, existing in the mythic patterns enfolded in our mundane experiences. They do this, because in each of our problems we can locate the absence of a god - the absence of a numinous metaphor that connects our problems to our culture.

Gods do not offer solutions to problems, they offer the problems reimagined. They're a way of seeing pathologies reformed as mythic, of healing the split between the individual and the collective through medicine of culture. They depersonalise problems, linking the individual to the psyche and to nature.

Gods are not a matter of faith, they do not care if you believe in them. They are a way of seeing and understanding the archetypal dimensions of the everyday, the patterns in the deeper narrative.

'The soul will fall sick again and again, until it gets what it needs,' wrote the psychologist James Hillman. In the same way, we find ourselves returning to the same haunts, and the same problems return in new ways, until we see through the details to the root of the issue, and discover what they really want to tell us.

So these poems act as markers of hauntings, things unseen that yet have power - the return of the gods through writing. They are metaphors for something half-known and half-felt, yet they are vital and filled with power to transform.

Perhaps we can learn to haunt ourselves, by allowing these disowned forces to reclaim their birthright: Both within the realm of our own haunted selves and the wider reality of our beautiful, haunted world.

Gods

'The gods have become diseases.'
- *Carl Jung*

The Ivy Covered Theatre

At the corner of North and New Street,
the theatre's bulk looms,
quiet as midnight.

Ornate sashes lead to
ebony balconies,
brickwork covered in ivy.

Ivy covers walls, roof-tiles, windows,
snakes around the banner that advertises
Waiting for Godot -
its tendrils stretch and burrow
into Lucky's ripped face.

In front of the empty box office,
black paving slabs
lit silver and green;
dead silence
in the ghosted street.

I walk around the building
where the rotten door swings
on rotten hinges,
push it open and
walk into its darkness,
the atmosphere as thick as a secret,
as heavy as a crown of ivy,
the ghosts of forgotten actors,
the shadowed hulk of the broken stage -

everywhere,
everywhere,
everywhere,

the snaking tendrils of
the green god's leaves.

Amulet

A speech by Hermes Trismagestus, god of theft, magic, business, language, guide of souls to the underworld, 'the most human of the gods'.

The path up is the path down...
The way back is the way onward...
Black is white and white is black...
The great secret is no secret...

Come closer and I will tell you.

Spend your time on this and that...
If you want mankind to be a brotherhood,
go out and meet your brothers!
If you want to sit in a room and split
words apart with a knife, do this.

Just remember -

when you cross the border -
to give your gold to me,

and I will be your Amulet.

For, in the coming time,
there will be no distinctions.
The shades of the dead
know not the colour they are,
so live now.

Know your wise heart,
your foolish heart,
your cunning heart,
your evil heart.

Know them all,
that you may give them to me
when you cross the border,

and I will be your Amulet.

Blue Flowers

Orpheus,
I missed you
at the poetry reading.

Each poet turned
in on their
own small
grief
as if trapped
in their living room.
None had the
burning torch
of Orpheus
for a pen.

Yet you,
whose grief
penetrated
that dark
chasm in Thrace,
who turned
at the threshold
of death
to face the
illusion
of your beloved's
blue lips -

You never again
mistook a poem
for a kiss.

So, make acceptances
when sorrow swamps
poetry,
the small comfort

of re-membering,
what's been dismembered;

When your ribs,
your hips
were torn to strips of meat
by jealous women,
your voice sang unbroken songs of
love and death.

The little blue
flowers that grow
by the river
swayed in the breeze,
made no comment.

Loves

'Life's an illusion, love is a dream.'
- *The Buzzcocks*

On A Hook (Re-membering Inanna)

'The true revolution begins in the individual who can be true to
his or her depression.'
- *James Hillman*

She seeks out her sister,
who lives in that dark
realm deep below
the tap root's stretch.

She descends, step by step,
through seven gates,
a pomegranate seed cake
held in her mouth.

At each gate she removes one
piece of clothing:
by the seventh
she is naked.

A golden boy, with
pale blue eyes,
kisses her tenderly,
lifts her up gently.

Hangs her on a hook,
like a puppy,
hanging
from her mother's mouth.

She hangs on that meat hook,
in the bowels of the earth
- the damp smell, the absence of stimulus -
waits to be remembered.

The taste of
seed cake in her mouth,
the kisses' memory
on her expectant lips.

The Bridge

Stillness on a bridge at midnight,
all's paused,
as if waiting
for a twig to crack,
or the moon to shine.

Night's palace,
an unfamiliar darkness,
wires the blood
with thin branches.

And perhaps God's a woman,
who kissed me twice:

Once in a crowded
room through the hidden agency
of some mortal's lips,
and again invisible, alone,
on this bridge.

The lichen exhales,
stillness passes,
light spills
from the crack
in a broken guitar.

Snake, Rose, Dance

'Glamour is a modern invention. Glamour cannot exist without
personal social envy being a common and widespread emotion.'
- *John Berger*

Mirror, candlestick, flame,
she stares at the flickering light,

reaches forwards, smiles,
as if anticipating some private moment of ecstasy.

She passes her hand over the flame,
sways slightly, then frowns,

red lips, white dress, dark eyes,
scent of artificial strawberries.

The candle goes out, a wisp of smoke,
the girl smiles again to the mirror,

she watches her reflection dance,
as she dances, slowly, hypnotically,

An enchanted blossom falls through space
on the swaying spine of a gold green snake.

Evaporations

I have collected these poems under the title *Evaporations*, because of the way they draw from daily life, dealing with the multiple impressions a person can give you, walking a path to Whitehawk Hill walked by your ancestors, thousands of years before.

Art, ecstasy and criticism

One of the frustrations I've had with art is the way it freezes moments into time, filling them full of meaning and emotion, until it seems that this is the most important thing in the world.

What then? I want to share it of course. I want to tell everyone to read Diana Wynne Jones's *Fire and Hemlock* or listen to Scott Walker's *Boy Child* or get tickets for Punchdrunk's *Firebird Ball* or see Hundertwasser's *Garden of the Happy Dead...*

I think the correct name for this feeling is ecstasy, a state of total union with its object. It's one reason that I am suspicious of critics, as they always seek to dissect that experience.

Of course, good criticism allows a deepening of this pleasure, and can be a work of art in itself, but - at its worst - it's more like an echo that puts forward a point of view as if it were a final judgement, keeping what is mysterious and moving in art within safe, rational lines.

Life flows on

Still, the moment of epiphany passes. It evaporates, life continues, the bills need paying, I've lost the lead to my camera, the laundry is piling up, the chimney is leaking, my job is under threat, cuts of public services, climate change...

Life itself seems like an evaporation too: it has form and reality, but it keeps going like a river.

A dream

The first poem, *Haunted Evaporation*, belongs, in some ways, in both sections of the book. It is an order: a voice saying:

'Not enough. Learn to become haunted.'

The poem was based on a dream, although the details are long-since forgotten. All I remember clearly is the urgency of the message, and that it was meant for me. It seemed to draw me back to think about real life.

'Not enough. Learn to become haunted.'

This means something to me, something like knowing the ephemerality of life and deeply living it at the same time in spite of illusion, transience and political despair.

Yes, all true, still.

'Not enough. Learn to become haunted.'

Underworlds

'Underworld is Psyche.'
- *James Hillman*

Haunted Evaporation

'As a lamp, a cataract, a star in space,
an illusion, a dewdrop, a bubble,
a dream, a cloud, a flash of lightning,
view all created things like this.'
- *Tathagate Buddha, The Diamond Sutra*

I learned to listen
until one ear grew to
half the side of my head.

Learn to become haunted

I learned that every thing
is alive - the rocks, the rain,
the gutters and drains,
even the grey marks stained
on blandly patterned carpets
in featureless Travelodges
have a moment of birth.

It's not enough

I learned my rage, my heart,
were bubbles
in the hand of a
distracted child,
they reflect and burst
leaving only the
dirty trace
of a rainbow.

Learn to become haunted

I learned my glamorous mind
was filled with chattering demons,
that the abandoned man

with the schizophrenic mother
and a skin
of dust and paint
was closer to god than
I,
that, as Jane's Addiction sing,
'How you treat the weak
is your true nature calling.'

Learn to become
haunted, haunted,
learn to become haunted -
as haunted as breath
when it enters
the body

I learned how to stop pretending
that my feelings were me,
I learned to stop defining myself
by my misery,
that my heroic attempts
to overcome suffering
just perpetuated them.

I learned of this world
and its paranoid core,
how the rational few
keep their mind in a jar,

I learned to slow down
and watch the pigeon
lady scattering cheap
bread to the birds in
the newly landscaped park,
to gaze stupidly
at fat pink
rhododendrons
nodding in the breeze,
to interpret graffiti on derelict churches,
to let bricks decay,

and to stop listening
to the hypnotic repetitions
of the newsreaders.

I learned that nature itself was
as changeable as a mood,
as temporary as a life,
as symbolic as clothing,
that there was no core, no essence,
only an endlesss stream of fantasies enacted
on a stage made up of slick institutions,
concrete streets and silenced stories,
tasteful corporate lobbies
and temporary accommodation.

I learned to question
all my thoughts,
to bargain with my fears,
to realise I was the same as everyone else,
that I was no better, no worse, no different,
that all my questions,
and poetry, were just ways of keeping
the black dog at bay -
of secretly crowning myself
king of an imaginary kingdom
that no one was permitted to enter,
near cracked housing
in isolated valleys, where
the only shop sells
happy shopper food -
taking refuge in the belief in an invisible
garden of high grass, green mazes, wildflowers
and broken statues.

Until the contradictions struck
my voice away,
and all I could do is gesture at the beauty,
the horror,
the terror,
and the pity,

You have learned how to listen,
but yet you repeat
all of the things you have learned
as if they might somehow accumulate
into something -
that you might possess
the sense of being a better person,
or a moment's weightlessness,
or some kind of moral superiority,
gained through insight into ephemerality.
But what if there were no one who learned all those things?
What if there was no kingdom, no bubble, no garden, and no one listening?

Learn to become
haunted, haunted,
learn to become haunted -
as haunted as breath
when it enters
the body,
a passing song
composed by
its own heart
in this sensual world,
with your ripe red heart,
in the green
dance of ecstasy
in the yellow moon
of sorrow.

Become what you are -
a ghost amongst ghosts -
learn to become
a haunted evaporation.

Red Stone

This longed-for
struggle
to make fire solid
anger
strong as wine
crystallised;
veins of ruby in
an uncut stone.

Four Aspects Of A Smile

You smiled at me,
blank and open,
with dazzling dumbness,
no siren, no allure.

Ten minutes later,
with you ten minutes behind me,
I looked again and saw four women
hidden in that smile's memory:

One gagged by shining metal -
she struggled desperately,
her dark eyes pleaded.

One wore a necklace of skulls,
claws for nails,
and a black widow grin.

One, a finance manager in
a two-piece pinstripe dress,
turned away,

Somewhere at the back,
a frightened little girl.

Haunted
Evaporations

'I greet you from the other side,
Of sorrow and despair,
With a love so vast and shattered,
It will reach you everywhere.'

- Leonard Cohen

The Wound And The Eye

I'll say a word: Sadness,
and give you a thorn in bloom,

the world and you seem tinted blue,
and filled with bitter perfume.

Sadness is a world you see,
the wound and the eye are the same,

reaching down to the chalky ground,
where the bones and the dust remain.

But sadness is only a word you see,
the world overspills the eye,

a dull warm ache, a need to relate,
confusion persists as to why.

So I'll say a word: Sadness,
but sadness is only a word,

beneath cement, a deep lament,
above it, the song of a bird.

'The wound and the eye are the same' is a quote from James Hillman, in the essay 'Intellectual Accompaniment by Two Fathers' by Watkins, Hillman and Friere.

Don't Tell Me About My Trauma Like That

For Marko Zlomovic and Steven Levine, with deep respect

Don't tell me about actors performing
Samuel Beckett in besieged Sarajevo,
or Oedipus extinguishing his eyes
on an ancient Greek stage,
while, for a thousand years, academics
and psychologists
make notes and compose theories
on the nature of the human soul.

Don't tell me that great works of art
will help me understand,
or that I must embrace chaos,
know the suffering,
and still say yes to life.

Your excitement about the vitality
of art in the face of trauma chills me.
It reminds me of the dull silence
that wrapped me
in putrid skin
as I looked at the countless
bodies heaped into graves
in Vukovar -
the small holes
in the children's skulls.

It was not great art or
literature that came to
relieve this deadness,
but a children's rhyme:

'Ashes, ashes,
We all fall down.'

You say that chaos is
part of the world
and gives it form.

I know this too much.

I want my freedom
to be found in occasional
translations of that
ghastly silence,
into small moments
of silent freedom
within mundane
tasks -

The shopping's
unpacked,
I'm up to my wrists
in a sink full of
soap and dishes,
then stopped
for a moment
by the water's heat...
as if this
moment's pause
was the true ground of being;
like the garden through
the window,
vibrant and still,
predictable,

alive.

Retrieval

I can walk a green path
from my house to Whitehawk Hill,
if I avoid the concrete,
step only on grass and soil.

It's 6,000 years
since men and women,
children and elders,
walked their own green path,
to arrive at this place where
earthworks meet sky,
cross chalkmarks that separate
the living from their ghosts.

A place of high corridors and night fire,
where life meets death in a
chalkwhite labyrinth,
overlooking the sea,
under wind and rain.

These people made a sanctuary to their own passing,
reshaped the landscape with that oldest human prayer,
broke the hold of roots and thorns,
and placed their symbol on the nested hill.

Now it's just
crumbled earth in a neglected field,
the track to the hospital
by the road to the estate,
a sometime gypsy camp
til they barred the edge with concrete posts,
resting place for butterflies and wildflowers -
yarrow, adonis, chalkhill blue.

The once gleaming earthworks
are collapsed ripples

in the mournful grass,
below the towering phone mast,
and the padlocked allotment's gate.

In the Twenties, archaeologists,
granted time to dig before the road was built,
found the footprint of two huge posts -
beneath one,
the upright skeleton of a stag,
beneath the other,
the remains of a child.

'They say you're remembered for three generations,'
says Colin, as I wait for my turn to use the tap
on the allotments that patchwork
the old hill now
(And then do we slip into the sea of forgottenness,
poppies dissolved in hot milk and lemon?)

Rosie Probert in Captain Cat's dream:
'Remember me.
I have forgotten you.
I am going into the darkness of the darkness for ever.'

I remember
the smell of cut grass, mint and terracotta
from the garden of my childhood -
how can I praise its retrieval's weird ache?

How it arises unbidden,
seeking remembrance,
the flesh of a ghost
stitched into a heart,
alert as a rabbit
on the edge of the thorns.

Mint grows in drifts here too,
hidden amongst these brambles;
light fades on shivering grass,
bones and ghosts rest

in forgotten chalk circles,
where the Downs bend into
bowbacked whales,
dive deep beneath the horizon's meniscus,
retrieve thin slices
of the dying
Electric Peach Sun.

'What is a ghost? A tragedy condemned to repeat itself time and again? An instant of pain, perhaps. Something dead which still seems to be alive. An emotion suspended in time. Like a blurred photograph. Like an insect trapped in amber.'
- *Guillermo del Toro, The Devil's Backbone, 2001*

Made in the USA
Columbia, SC
26 January 2018